SELECTED POEMS

FEATURING SELECTIONS FROM THE BOOK OF
IMAGES, THE BOOK OF HOURS, & MORE

RAINER MARIA RILKE

D1714500

Translated by
JESSIE LEMONT

CONTENTS

EXCERPTS FROM NEW
POEMS

EXCERPTS FROM THE BOOK
OF HOURS

EXCERPTS FROM FIRST POEMS

EVENING

The bleak fields are asleep,
My heart alone wakes;
The evening in the harbour
Down his red sails takes.

Night, guardian of dreams,
Now wanders through the land;
The moon, a lily white,
Blossoms within her hand.

MARY VIRGIN

How came, how came from out thy
    night
Mary, so much light
And so much gloom:
Who was thy bridegroom?

Thou callest, thou callest and thou hast
    forgot
That thou the same art not
Who came to me
In thy Virginity.

I am still so blossoming, so young.
How shall I go on tiptoe
From childhood to Annunciation
Through the dim twilight
Into thy Garden.

EXCERPTS FROM THE
BOOK OF IMAGES

PRESAGING

I am like a flag unfurled in space,
I scent the oncoming winds and must
    bend with them,
While the things beneath are not yet
    stirring,
While doors close gently and there is
    silence in the chimneys
And the windows do not yet tremble
    and the dust is still heavy—
Then I feel the storm and am vibrant
    like the sea
And expand and withdraw into myself
And thrust myself forth and am alone
    in the great storm.

AUTUMN

The leaves fall, fall as from far,
Like distant gardens withered in the
    heavens;
They fall with slow and lingering
    descent.

And in the nights the heavy Earth, too,
    falls
From out the stars into the Solitude.

Thus all doth fall. This hand of mine
    must fall
And lo! the other one:—it is the law.
But there is One who holds this falling
Infinitely softly in His hands.

SILENT HOUR

Whoever weeps somewhere out in the
    world
Weeps without cause in the world
Weeps over me.

Whoever laughs somewhere out in the
    night
Laughs without cause in the night
Laughs at me.

Whoever wanders somewhere in the
    world
Wanders in vain in the world
Wanders to me.

Whoever dies somewhere in the world
Dies without cause in the world
Looks at me.

THE ANGELS

They all have tired mouths
And luminous, illimitable souls;
And a longing (as if for sin)
Trembles at times through their
    dreams.

They all resemble one another,
In God's garden they are silent
Like many, many intervals
In His mighty melody.

But when they spread their wings
They awaken the winds
That stir as though God
With His far-reaching master hands
Turned the pages of the dark book of
    Beginning.

SOLITUDE

Solitude is like a rain
That from the sea at dusk begins to
    rise;
It floats remote across the far-off plain
Upward into its dwelling-place, the
    skies,
Then o'er the town it slowly sinks
    again.
Like rain it softly falls at that dim hour
When ghostly lanes turn toward the
    shadowy morn;
When bodies weighed with satiate
    passion's power
Sad, disappointed from each other
    turn;
When men with quiet hatred burning
    deep

Together in a common bed must
    sleep—
Through the gray, phantom shadows
    of the dawn
Lo! Solitude floats down the river wan
    ...

KINGS IN LEGENDS

Kings in old legends seem
Like mountains rising in the evening
    light.
They blind all with their gleam,
Their loins encircled are by girdles
    bright,
Their robes are edged with bands
Of precious stones—the rarest earth
    affords—
With richly jeweled hands
They hold their slender, shining, naked
    swords.

THE KNIGHT

The Knight rides forth in coat of mail
Into the roar of the world.
And here is Life: the vines in the vale
And friend and foe, and the feast in the
    hall,
And May and the maid, and the glen
    and the grail;
God's flags afloat on every wall
In a thousand streets unfurled.

Beneath the armour of the Knight
Behind the chain's black links
Death crouches and thinks and thinks:
"When will the sword's blade sharp
    and bright
Forth from the scabbard spring
And cut the network of the cloak

Enmeshing me ring on ring—
When will the foe's delivering stroke
Set me free
To dance
And sing?"

THE BOY

I wish I might become like one of
    these
Who, in the night on horses wild
    astride,
With torches flaming out like loosened
    hair
On to the chase through the great swift
    wind ride.
I wish to stand as on a boat and dare
The sweeping storm, mighty, like flag
    unrolled
In darkness but with helmet made
    of gold
That shimmers restlessly. And in a row,
Behind me in the dark, ten men
    that glow
With helmets that are restless, too, like
    mine,

Now old and dull, now clear as glass
    they shine.
One stands by me and blows a blast
    apace
On his great flashing trumpet and the
    sound
Shrieks through the vast black solitude
    around
Through which, as through a wild mad
    dream we race.
The houses fall behind us on their
    knees,
Before us bend the streets and them we
    gain,
The great squares yield to us and them
    we seize—
And on our steeds rush like the roar of
    rain.

INITIATION

Whosoever thou art! Out in the
    evening roam,
Out from thy room thou know'st in
    every part,
And far in the dim distance leave thy
    home,
Whosoever thou art.
Lift thine eyes which lingering see
The shadows on the foot-worn
    threshold fall,
Lift thine eyes slowly to the great
    dark tree
That stands against heaven, solitary,
    tall,
And thou hast visioned Life, its
    meanings rise
Like words that in the silence clearer
    grow;

As they unfold before thy will to know
Gently withdraw thine eyes—

THE NEIGHBOUR

Strange violin! Dost thou follow me?
In many foreign cities, far away,
Thy lone voice spoke to me like
      memory.
Do hundreds play thee, or does but
      one play?

Are there in all great cities tempest-
      tossed
Men who would seek the rivers but for
      thee,

Who, but for thee, would be forever
      lost?
Why drifts thy lonely voice always
      to me?
Why am I the neighbour always

Of those who force to sing thy
    trembling strings?
Life is more heavy—thy song says—
Than the vast, heavy burden of all
    things.

SONG OF THE STATUE

Who so loveth me that he
Will give his precious life for me?
I shall be set free from the stone
If some one drowns for me in the sea,
I shall have life, life of my own,—
For life I ache.

I long for the singing blood,
The stone is so still and cold.
I dream of life, life is good.
Will no one love me and be bold
And me awake?

.   .   .   .

I weep and weep alone,
Weep always for my stone.

What joy is my blood to me
If it ripens like red wine?
It cannot call back from the sea
The life that was given for mine,
Given for Love's sake.

MAIDENS. I

Others must by a long dark way
Stray to the mystic bards,
Or ask some one who has heard
    them sing
Or touch the magic chords.
Only the maidens question not
The bridges that lead to Dream;
Their luminous smiles are like strands
    of pearls
On a silver vase agleam.

The maidens' doors of Life lead out
Where the song of the poet soars,
And out beyond to the great world—
To the world beyond the doors.

MAIDENS. II

Maidens the poets learn from you
     to tell
How solitary and remote you are,
As night is lighted by one high
     bright star
They draw light from the distance
     where you dwell.

For poet you must always maiden be
Even though his eyes the woman in
     you wake
Wedding brocade your fragile wrists
     would break,
Mysterious, elusive, from him flee.

Within his garden let him wait alone
Where benches stand expectant in the
     shade

Within the chamber where the lyre was
    played
Where he received you as the eternal
    One.

Go! It grows dark—your voice and
    form no more
His senses seek; he now no longer sees
A white robe fluttering under dark
    beech trees
Along the pathway where it gleamed
    before.

He loves the long paths where no
    footfalls ring,
And he loves much the silent chamber
    where
Like a soft whisper through the
    quiet air
He hears your voice, far distant,
    vanishing.

The softly stealing echo comes again
From crowds of men whom, wearily,
    he shuns;
And many see you there—so his
    thought runs—
And tenderest memories are pierced
    with pain.

THE BRIDE

Call me, Beloved! Call aloud to me!
Thy bride her vigil at the window
    keeps;
The evening wanes to dusk, the
    dimness creeps
Down empty alleys of the old plane-
    tree.

O! Let thy voice enfold me close about,
Or from this dark house, lonely and
    remote,
Through deep blue gardens where
    gray shadows float
I will pour forth my soul with hands
    stretched out ...

AUTUMNAL DAY

Lord! It is time. So great was
    Summer's glow:
Thy shadows lay upon the dials' faces
And o'er wide spaces let thy tempests
    blow.

Command to ripen the last fruits of
    thine,
Give to them two more burning days
    and press
The last sweetness into the heavy wine.

He who has now no house will ne'er
    build one,
Who is alone will now remain alone;
He will awake, will read, will letters
    write

Through the long day and in the
    lonely night;
And restless, solitary, he will rove
Where the leaves rustle, wind-blown, in
    the grove.

MOONLIGHT NIGHT

South-German night! the ripe moon
    hangs above
Weaving enchantment o'er the
    shadowy lea.
From the old tower the hours fall
    heavily
Into the dark as though into the sea—
A rustle, a call of night-watch in the
    grove,
Then for a while void silence fills
    the air;
And then a violin (from God knows
    where)
Awakes and slowly sings: Oh Love ...
    Oh Love ...

IN APRIL

Again the woods are odorous, the lark
Lifts on upsoaring wings the
    heaven gray
That hung above the tree-tops, veiled
    and dark,
Where branches bare disclosed the
    empty day.

After long rainy afternoons an hour
Comes with its shafts of golden light
    and flings
Them at the windows in a radiant
    shower,
And rain drops beat the panes like
    timorous wings.

Then all is still. The stones are crooned
    to sleep

By the soft sound of rain that slowly
    dies;
And cradled in the branches,
    hidden deep
In each bright bud, a slumbering
    silence lies.

MEMORIES OF A CHILDHOOD

The darkness hung like richness in
    the room
When like a dream the mother entered
    there
And then a glass's tinkle stirred the air
Near where a boy sat in the silent
    gloom.

The room betrayed the mother—so
    she felt—
She kissed her boy and questioned
    "Are you here?"
And with a gesture that he held
    most dear
Down for a moment by his side she
    knelt.

Toward the piano they both shyly
    glanced
For she would sing to him on many a
    night,
And the child seated in the fading light
Would listen strangely as if half
    entranced,

His large eyes fastened with a
    quiet glow
Upon the hand which by her ring
    seemed bent
And slowly wandering o'er the white
    keys went
Moving as though against a drift of
    snow.

DEATH

Before us great Death stands
Our fate held close within his quiet
    hands.
When with proud joy we lift Life's
    red wine
To drink deep of the mystic
    shining cup
And ecstasy through all our being
    leaps—
Death bows his head and weeps.

THE ASHANTEE

(Jardin d'Acclimatation, Paris)

No vision of exotic southern countries,
No dancing women, supple, brown
    and tall
Whirling from out their falling
    draperies
To melodies that beat a fierce mad call;

No sound of songs that from the hot
    blood rise,
No langorous, stretching, dusky, velvet
    maids
Flashing like gleaming weapon their
    bright eyes,
No swift, wild thrill the quickening
    blood pervades.

Only mouths widening with a still
  broad smile
Of comprehension, a strange knowing
  leer
At white men, at their vanity and guile,
An understanding that fills one with
  fear.

The beasts in cages much more
  loyal are,
Restlessly pacing, pacing to and fro,
Dreaming of countries beckoning from
  afar,
Lands where they roamed in days of
  long ago.

They burn with an unquenched and
  smothered fire
Consumed by longings over which they
  brood,
Oblivious of time, without desire,
Alone and lost in their great solitude.

REMEMBRANCE

Expectant and waiting you muse
On the great rare thing which alone
To enhance your life you would
    choose:
The awakening of the stone,
The deeps where yourself you would
    lose.

In the dusk of the shelves, embossed
Shine the volumes in gold and browns,
And you think of countries once
    crossed,
Of pictures, of shimmering gowns
Of the women that you have lost.

And it comes to you then at last—
And you rise for you are aware

Of a year in the far off past
With its wonder and fear and prayer.

MUSIC

What play you, O Boy? Through the
    garden it stole
Like wandering steps, like a whisper—
    then mute;
What play you, O Boy? Lo! your
    gypsying soul
Is caught and held fast in the pipes of
    Pan's flute.

And what conjure you? Imprisoned is
    the song,
It lingers and longs in the reeds where
    it lies;
Your young life is strong, but how
    much more strong
Is the longing that through your music
    sighs.

Let your flute be still and your soul
    float through
Waves of sound formless as waves of
    the sea,
For here your song lived and it
    wisely grew
Before it was forced into melody.

Its wings beat gently, its note no more
    calls,
Its flight has been spent by you,
    dreaming Boy!
Now it no longer steals over my
    walls—
But in my garden I'd woo it to joy.

MAIDEN MELANCHOLY

A young knight comes into my mind
As from some myth of old.

He came! You felt yourself entwined
As a great storm would round you
    wind.
He went! A blessing undefined
Seemed left, as when church-bells
    declined
And left you wrapt in prayer.
You fain would cry aloud—but bind
Your scarf about you and tear-blind
Weep softly in its fold.

A young knight comes into my mind
Full armored forth to fare.

His smile was luminously kind

Like glint of ivory enshrined,
Like a home longing undivined,
Like Christmas snows where dark ways
    wind,
Like sea-pearls about turquoise twined,
Like moonlight silver when combined
With a loved book's rare gold.

MAIDENS AT CONFIRMATION

(Paris in May, 1903)

The white veiled maids to
    confirmation go
Through deep green garden paths they
    slowly wind;
Their childhood they are leaving now
    behind:
The future will be different, they know.

Oh! Will it come? They wait—It must
    come soon!
The next long hour slowly strikes at
    last,
The whole house stirs again, the feast
    is past,
And sadly passes by the afternoon ...

Like resurrection were the garments
    white
The wreathed procession walked
    through trees arched wide
Into the church, as cool as silk inside,
With long aisles of tall candles flaming
    bright:
The lights all shone like jewels rich
    and rare
To solemn eyes that watched them
    gleam and flare.

Then through the silence the great
    song rose high
Up to the vaulted dome like clouds it
    soared,
Then luminously, gently down it
    poured—
Over white veils like rain it seemed
    to die.

The wind through the white garments
    softly stirred
And they grew vari-coloured in
    each fold
And each fold hidden blossoms seemed
    to hold
And flowers and stars and fluting notes
    of bird,

And dim, quaint figures shimmering
    like gold
Seemed to come forth from distant
    myths of old.

Outside the day was one of green and
    blue,
With touches of a luminous glowing
    red,
Across the quiet pond the small waves
    sped.
Beyond the city, gardens hidden
    from view
Sent odors of sweet blossoms on the
    breeze
And singing sounded through the far
    off trees.

It was as though garlands crowned
    everything
And all things were touched softly by
    the sun;
And many windows opened one
    by one
And the light trembled on them
    glistening.

THE WOMAN WHO LOVES

Ah yes! I long for you. To you I glide
And lose myself—for to you I belong.
The hope that hitherto I have denied
Imperious comes to me as from
    your side
Serious, unfaltering and swift and
    strong.

Those times: the times when I was
    quite alone
By memories wrapt that whispered to
    me low,
My silence was the quiet of a stone
Over which rippling murmuring
    waters flow.

But in these weeks of the awakening
    Spring

Something within me has been freed
    —something
That in the past dark years
    unconscious lay,
Which rises now within me and
    commands
And gives my poor warm life into your
    hands
Who know not what I was that
    Yesterday.

PONT DU CARROUSEL

Upon the bridge the blind man stands
    alone,
Gray like a mist veiled monument he
    towers
As though of nameless realms the
    boundary stone
About which circle distant starry
    hours.

He seems the center around which
    stars glow
While all earth's ostentations surge
    below.

Immovably and silently he stands
Placed where the confused current
    ebbs and flows;

Past fathomless dark depths that he
    commands
A shallow generation drifting goes....

MADNESS

She thinks: I am—Have you not seen?
Who are you then, Marie?
I am a Queen, I am a Queen!
To your knee, to your knee!

And then she weeps: I was—a child—
Who were you then, Marie?
Know you that I was no man's child,
Poor and in rags—said she.

And then a Princess I became
To whom men bend their knees;
To princes things are not the same
As those a beggar sees.

And those things which have made you
    great
Came to you, tell me, when?

One night, one night, one night quite
    late,
Things became different then.

I walked the lane which presently
With strung chords seemed to bend;
Then Marie became Melody
And danced from end to end.

The people watched with startled mien
And passed with frightened glance
For all know that only a Queen
May dance in the lanes: dance!...

LAMENT

Oh! All things are long passed away
    and far.
A light is shining but the distant star
From which it still comes to me has
    been dead
A thousand years ... In the dim
    phantom boat
That glided past some ghastly thing
    was said.
A clock just struck within some house
    remote.
Which house?—I long to still my
    beating heart.
Beneath the sky's vast dome I long to
    pray ...
Of all the stars there must be far away
A single star which still exists apart.

And I believe that I should know
    the one
Which has alone endured and which
    alone
Like a white City that all space
    commands
At the ray's end in the high heaven
    stands.

SYMBOLS

From infinite longings finite deeds rise
As fountains spring toward far-off
    glowing skies,
But rushing swiftly upward
    weakly bend
And trembling from their lack of
    power descend—
So through the falling torrent of our
    fears
Our joyous force leaps like these
    dancing tears.

EXCERPTS FROM NEW
POEMS

EARLY APOLLO

As when at times there breaks through
    branches bare
A morning vibrant with the breath of
    spring,
About this poet-head a splendour rare
Transforms it almost to a mortal thing.

There is as yet no shadow in his
    glance,
Too cool his temples for the laurel's
    glow;
But later o'er those marble brows,
    perchance,
A rose-garden with bushes tall will
    grow,

And single petals one by one will fall

O'er the still mouth and break its silent
    thrall,
—The mouth that trembles with a
    dawning smile
As though a song were rising there the
    while.

THE TOMB OF A YOUNG GIRL

We still remember! The same as
    of yore
All that has happened once again
    must be.
As grows a lemon-tree upon the
    shore—
It was like that—your light, small
    breasts you bore,
And his blood's current coursed like
    the wild sea.

That god—
who was the wanderer, the slim
Despoiler of fair women; he—the wise,
    —

But sweet and glowing as your
    thoughts of him

Who cast a shadow over your
    young limb
While bending like your arched brows
    o'er your eyes.

THE POET

You Hour! From me you ever take your
    flight,
Your swift wings wound me as they
    whir along;
Without you void would be my day
    and night,
Without you I'll not capture my great
    song.

I have no earthly spot where I can live,
I have no love, I have no household
    fane,
And all the things to which myself
    I give
Impoverish me with richness they
    attain.

THE PANTHER

His weary glance, from passing by the
    bars,
Has grown into a dazed and vacant
    stare;
It seems to him there are a thousand
    bars
And out beyond those bars the
    empty air.

The pad of his strong feet, that
    ceaseless sound
Of supple tread behind the iron bands,
Is like a dance of strength circling
    around,
While in the circle, stunned, a great
    will stands.

But there are times the pupils of
    his eyes
Dilate, the strong limbs stand alert,
    apart,
Tense with the flood of visions that
    arise
Only to sink and die within his heart.

GROWING BLIND

Among all the others there sat a guest
Who sipped her tea as if one apart,
And she held her cup not quite like the
    rest;
Once she smiled so it pierced one's
    heart.

When the group of people arose at last
And laughed and talked in a merry
    tone,
As lingeringly through the rooms they
    passed
I saw that she followed alone.

Tense and still like one who to sing
    must rise
Before a throng on a festal night

She lifted her head, and her bright
    glad eyes
Were like pools which reflected light.

She followed on slowly after the last
As though some object must be
    passed by,
And yet as if were it once but passed
She would no longer walk but fly.

THE SPANISH DANCER

As a lit match first flickers in the hands
Before it flames, and darts out from all
    sides
Bright, twitching tongues, so, ringed by
    growing bands
Of spectators—she, quivering, glowing
    stands
Poised tensely for the dance—then
    forward glides

And suddenly becomes a flaming
    torch.
Her bright hair flames, her burning
    glances scorch,
And with a daring art at her command
Her whole robe blazes like a fire-brand
From which is stretched each naked
    arm, awake,

Gleaming and rattling like a frightened
    snake.

And then, as though the fire fainter
    grows,
She gathers up the flame—again it
    glows,
As with proud gesture and imperious
    air
She flings it to the earth; and it lies
    there
Furiously flickering and crackling
    still—
Then haughtily victorious, but with
    sweet
Swift smile of greeting, she puts forth
    her will
And stamps the flames out with her
    small firm feet.

OFFERING

My body glows in every vein and
    blooms
To fullest flower since I first knew thee,
My walk unconscious pride and power
    assumes;
Who art thou then—thou who awaitest
    me?

When from the past I draw myself the
    while
I lose old traits as leaves of autumn
    fall;
I only know the radiance of thy smile,
Like the soft gleam of stars,
    transforming all.

Through childhood's years I wandered
    unaware

Of shimmering visions my thoughts
    now arrests
To offer thee, as on an altar fair
That's lighted by the bright flame of
    thy hair
And wreathéd by the blossoms of thy
    breasts.

LOVE SONG

When my soul touches yours a great
    chord sings!
How shall I tune it then to other
    things?
O! That some spot in darkness could
    be found
That does not vibrate whene'er your
    depths sound.
But everything that touches you
    and me
Welds us as played strings sound one
    melody.
Where is the instrument whence the
    sounds flow?
And whose the master-hand that holds
    the bow?
O! Sweet song—

ARCHAIC TORSO OF APOLLO

We cannot fathom his mysterious
    head,
Through the veiled eyes no flickering
    ray is sent:
But from his torso gleaming light
    is shed
As from a candelabrum; inward bent
His glance there glows and lingers.
    Otherwise
The round breast would not blind you
    with its grace,
Nor could the soft-curved circle of the
    thighs
Steal to the arc whence issues a new
    race.
Nor could this stark and stunted stone
    display

Vibrance beneath the shoulders
    heavy bar,
Nor shine like fur upon a beast of
    prey,
Nor break forth from its lines like a
    great star—
There is no spot that does not bind
    you fast
And transport you back, back to a far
    past.

EXCERPTS FROM THE
BOOK OF HOURS

THE BOOK OF A MONK'S LIFE

I live my life in circles that grow wide
And endlessly unroll,
I may not reach the last, but on I glide
Strong pinioned toward my goal.

About the old tower, dark against
    the sky,
The beat of my wings hums,
I circle about God, sweep far and high
On through milleniums.

Am I a bird that skims the clouds
    along,
Or am I a wild storm, or a great song?

Many have painted her. But there
    was one

Who drew his radiant colours from
    the sun.
Mysteriously glowing through a
    background dim
When he was suffering she came
    to him,
And all the heavy pain within his heart
Rose in his hands and stole into his art.
His canvas is the beautiful bright veil
Through which her sorrow shines.
    There where the
Texture o'er her sad lips is closely
    drawn
A trembling smile softly begins to dawn
    ...
Though angels with seven candles light
    the place
You cannot read the secret of her face.

In cassocks clad I have had many
    brothers
In southern cloisters where the laurel
    grows,
They paint Madonnas like fair human
    mothers
And I dream of young Titians and of
    others
In which the God with shining
    radiance glows.

But though my vigil constantly I keep
My God is dark—like woven texture
    flowing,
A hundred drinking roots, all
    intertwined;
I only know that from His warmth I'm
    growing.
More I know not: my roots lie
    hidden deep
My branches only are swayed by the
    wind.

Thou Anxious One! And dost thou
    then not hear
Against thee all my surging senses sing?
About thy face in circles drawing near
My thought floats like a fluttering
    white wing.

Dost thou not see, before thee stands
    my soul
In silence wrapt my Springtime's
    prayer to pray?
But when thy glance rests on me then
    my whole
Being quickens and blooms like trees
    in May.

When thou art dreaming then I am thy
    Dream,

But when thou art awake I am thy Will
Potent with splendour, radiant and
    sublime,
Expanding like far space star-lit and
    still
Into the distant mystic realm of Time.

I love my life's dark hours
In which my senses quicken and grow
    deep,
While, as from faint incense of faded
    flowers
Or letters old, I magically steep
Myself in days gone by: again I give
Myself unto the past:—again I live.

Out of my dark hours wisdom dawns
    apace,
Infinite Life unrolls its boundless space
    ...

Then I am shaken as a sweeping storm
Shakes a ripe tree that grows above a
    grave
'Round whose cold clay the roots twine
    fast and warm—
And Youth's fair visions that glowed
    bright and brave,
Dreams that were closely cherished
    and for long,

Are lost once more in sadness and in
    song.

By day Thou are the Legend and the
    Dream
That like a whisper floats about
    all men,
The deep and brooding stillnesses
    which seem,
After the hour has struck, to close
    again.

And when the day with drowsy gesture
    bends
And sinks to sleep beneath the evening
    skies,
As from each roof a tower of smoke
    ascends—
So does Thy Realm, my God, around
    me rise.

All those who seek Thee tempt Thee,
And those who find would bind Thee
To gesture and to form.

But I would comprehend Thee
As the wide Earth unfolds Thee.
Thou growest with my maturity,
Thou Art in calm and storm.

I ask of Thee no vanity
To evidence and prove Thee.
Thou Wert in eons old.

Perform no miracles for me,
But justify Thy laws to me
Which, as the years pass by me.
All soundlessly unfold.

In a house was one who arose from the
    feast
And went forth to wander in distant
    lands,
Because there was somewhere far off
    in the East
A spot which he sought where a great
    Church stands.
And ever his children, when breaking
    their bread,
Thought of him and rose up and
    blessed him as dead.

In another house was the one who had
    died,
Who still sat at table and drank from
    the glass
And ever within the walls did abide—
For out of the house he could no more
    pass.
And his children set forth to seek for
    the spot
Where stands the great Church which
    he forgot.

Extinguish my eyes, I still can see you,
Close my ears, I can hear your
    footsteps fall,
And without feet I still can follow you,
And without voice I still can to you
    call.
Break off my arms, and I can embrace
    you,
Enfold you with my heart as with a
    hand.
Hold my heart, my brain will take fire
    of you
As flax ignites from a lit fire-brand—
And flame will sweep in a swift rushing
    flood
Through all the singing currents of my
    blood.

In the deep nights I dig for you, O
　　Treasure!
To seek you over the wide world I
　　roam,
For all abundance is but meager
　　measure
Of your bright beauty which is yet to
　　come.

Over the road to you the leaves are
　　blowing,
Few follow it, the way is long and
　　steep.
You dwell in solitude—Oh, does your
　　glowing
Heart in some far off valley lie asleep?

My bloody hands, with digging
　　bruised, I've lifted,
Spread like a tree I stretch them in
　　the air
To find you before day to night has
　　drifted;
I reach out into space to seek you there
　　...

Then, as though with a swift impatient
　　gesture,
Flashing from distant stars on
　　sweeping wing,

You come, and over earth a magic
    vesture
Steals gently as the rain falls in the
    spring.

THE BOOK OF POVERTY AND DEATH

Her mouth is like the mouth of a
    fine bust
That cannot utter sound, nor breathe,
    nor kiss,
But that had once from Life received
    all this
Which shaped its subtle curves, and
    ever must
From fullness of past knowledge dwell
    alone,
A thing apart, a parable in stone.

Alone Thou wanderest through space,
Profound One with the hidden face;
Thou art Poverty's great rose,
The eternal metamorphose
Of gold into the light of sun.

Thou art the mystic homeless One;
Into the world Thou never came,
Too mighty Thou, too great to name;
Voice of the storm, Song that the wild
    wind sings,
Thou Harp that shatters those who
    play Thy strings!

A watcher of Thy spaces make me,
Make me a listener at Thy stone,
Give to me vision and then wake me
Upon Thy oceans all alone.
Thy rivers' courses let me follow
Where they leap the crags in their
    flight
And where at dusk in caverns hollow
They croon to music of the night.
Send me far into Thy barren land
Where the snow clouds the wild wind
    drives,
Where monasteries like gray shrouds
    stand—
August symbols of unlived lives.
There pilgrims climb slowly one
    by one,
And behind them a blind man goes:
With him I will walk till day is done
Up the pathway that no one knows ...

Made in the USA
Middletown, DE
02 February 2024